THOUGHTS FOR YOUNG MEN

J. C. Ryle

THE BANNER OF TRUTH TRUST

THE BANNER OF TRUTH TRUST

Head Office
3 Murrayfield Road
Edinburgh
EH12 6EL
UK

North America Sales
PO Box 621
Carlisle
PA 17013
USA

banneroftruth.org

Reproduced from J. C. Ryle,
The Upper Room (Wm Hunt & Co., 1888)
© The Banner of Truth Trust 2015

Reprinted 2016
Reprinted 2016
Reprinted 2018

*

ISBN
Print: 978 1 84871 652 0
EPUB: 978 1 84871 653 7
Kindle: 978 1 84871 654 4

*

Typeset in 11/15 Adobe Garamond Pro
at The Banner of Truth Trust, Edinburgh

Printed in the USA by
Versa Press Inc.,
East Peoria, IL.

Contents

Foreword

J. C. Ryle was a Mr Standfast during the shifting decades of the nineteenth century. As his denomination (the Church of England) was torn by movements to undo the Reformation—some by pulling back to Rome, others by pulling over into increasing unbelief—Ryle stood fast as a proponent of the old paths of biblical Christianity. He was a local pastor for decades, and then spent the last twenty years of his life as the first Bishop of Liverpool. During his long pastoral ministry many of his sermons and addresses were printed in their hundreds of thousands and were widely read to the great benefit of large numbers inside the Church of England and beyond.

Toward the end of his life, Ryle pulled together twenty-one of his 'sermons, addresses, lectures and tracts' and published them as *The Upper Room* (1888). He thought that they might survive and do more good bound together in a book than they would if left to fend for themselves. As wise as that decision was, the publisher now thinks that it is time to make at least one more of these addresses available as a separate, inexpensive paperback. As good as the other addresses in *The Upper Room* are, 'Thoughts for Young Men' is surely among the first rank in terms of its extraordinary usefulness.

Although delivered more than 130 years ago, 'Thoughts for Young Men' is strikingly contemporary. One might think that time changes most those who most reflect its changes. Trends and fads hold sway more tightly among the young. They come out of nowhere. They are taken up by almost everyone. Their rule is absolute—and short. Soon, one fad gives way to the next. What is fashionable among fifteen-year-olds this year will almost certainly not be in five years' time. With such a tendency to change seemingly built into the DNA of young people, the contemporary feel and timeliness of this nineteenth-century exhortation is all the more striking.

Beginning with Paul's exhortation to Titus in Titus 2:6 to be 'sober-minded', Ryle dispels, reminds, and exhorts. He dispels lies about the temptations young men faced then. And those same lies young men face today. Ryle dispels the myth that young men are strong. Strong bodies too often go with weak wills. He reminds young men that they face a real enemy whom they almost always forget. And, based on all of this, Ryle exhorts as only a seasoned, loving pastor can.

I remember reading this address recently, having not read it for decades, and being struck once again by the timelessness of Ryle's approach. If I did not know any better I could easily have concluded that it had been written only yesterday!

The body of the address is composed of four sections:

1. Reasons why young men need to be exhorted;

2. Dangers young men face;

3. Counsels (more general principles);

4. 'Special rules' for young men.

Of course, much of this book is as applicable for women as for men, and for the old as for the young; but it has a very special application to young men. I read much of it to several young men in our church recently, and they were surprised at how directly Ryle's counsels applied to their own situations.

Authors guide us through stories, but non-fiction works are best read differently. Ryle does not write to entertain but to instruct. To that end, let me conclude by simply giving the author's argument in outline form. Seeing what is coming next will help you read this book with greater profit, especially if you will humbly and prayerfully prepare your heart beforehand. Here, then, is the outline of the body of Ryle's address:

1. Five Reasons for Exhorting Young Men

    (1) There are few young men who seem to have any religion.

    (2) Death and judgment are before young men, even as others, and they nearly all seem to forget it.

    (3) What young men will be, in all probability depends on what they are now.

    (4) The devil uses special diligence to destroy the souls of young men, and they seem not to know it.

    (5) Young men need exhorting because of the sorrow it will save them, to begin serving God now.

2. *Five Special Dangers Young Men Need To Be Warned Against*
   (1) Pride.
   (2) The love of pleasure.
   (3) Thoughtlessness and inconsideration.
   (4) Contempt of religion.
   (5) The fear of man's opinion.

3. *Six General Counsels to Young Men*
   (1) Try to get a clear view of the evil of sin.
   (2) Seek to become acquainted with our Lord Jesus Christ.
   (3) Never forget that nothing is as important as your soul.
   (4) Never forget that it is possible to be a young man and to serve God.
   (5) Determine as long as you live to make the Bible your guide and adviser.
   (6) Never make an intimate friend of anyone who is not a friend of God. [Yes, you read that right. Read this section carefully and observe Ryle's wisdom here for our worldly age.]

4. *Five Special Rules for Young Men*
   (1) Resolve at once, by God's help, to break off every known sin, however small.
   (2) Resolve, by God's help, to shun everything which may prove an occasion of sin.
   (3) Resolve never to forget the eye of God is upon you.
   (4) Be diligent in the use of all public means of grace.
   (5) Resolve that wherever you are, you will pray.

Reader, I've detained you long enough. Prayerfully and urgently read, consider, and apply to your own life what our departed brother and pastor has to teach us for our own good and for God's greater glory.

MARK DEVER
Washington DC,
August 2015

Introduction

When St Paul wrote his Epistle to Titus about his duty as a minister, he mentioned young men as a class requiring peculiar attention. After speaking of aged men and aged women, and young women, he adds this pithy advice,—'Young men likewise exhort to be sober minded' (Titus 2:6). I am going to follow the apostle's advice. I propose to offer a few words of friendly exhortation to young men.

I am growing old myself, but there are few things I remember so well as the days of my youth. I have a most distinct recollection of the joys and the sorrows, the hopes and the fears, the temptations and the difficulties, the mistaken judgments and the misplaced affections, the errors and the aspirations, which surround and accompany a young man's life. If I can only say something to keep some young man in the right way, and preserve him from faults and sins, which may mar his prospects both for time and eternity, I shall be very thankful.

There are four things which I propose to do:—

1. I will mention some general *reasons* why young men need exhorting.

2. I will notice some special *dangers* against which young men need to be warned.

3. I will give some general *counsels*, which I entreat young men to receive.

4. I will set down some special *rules of conduct*, which I strongly advise young men to follow.

On each of these four points I have something to say, and I pray God that what I say may do good to some soul.

Part One

General Reasons for Exhorting Young Men

1. In the first place, *What are the general reasons why young men need peculiar exhortation?*

I will mention several of them in order.

(1) For one thing, there is the painful fact that *there are few young men anywhere who seem to have any religion.*

I speak without respect of persons; I say it of all. High or low, rich or poor, gentle or simple, learned or unlearned, in town or in country,—it makes no matter. I tremble to observe how few young men are led by the Spirit,—how few are in that narrow way which leads to life,—how few are setting their affections upon things above,—how few are taking up the cross, and following Christ. I say it with all sorrow, but I believe, as in God's sight, I am saying nothing more than the truth.

Young men, you form a large and most important class in the population of this country; but where, and in what condition, are your immortal souls? Alas, whatever way we turn for an answer, the report will be one and the same!

Let us ask any faithful minister of the gospel and mark what he will tell us. How many unmarried young people can he reckon up who come to the Lord's Supper? Who are the most backward about means of grace,—the most irregular about Sunday services,—the most difficult to draw to weekly lectures and prayer-meetings,—the most inattentive under preaching at all times? Which part of his congregation fills him with most anxiety? Who are the Reubens for whom he has the deepest 'searchings of heart'? Who in his flock are the hardest to manage,—who require the most frequent warnings and rebukes,—who occasion him the greatest uneasiness and sorrow,—who keep him most constantly in fear for their souls, and seem most hopeless? Depend on it, his answer will always be, *'The Young Men.'*

Let us ask the parents in any parish throughout England, and see what they will generally say. Who in their families give them most pain and trouble? Who need the most watchfulness, and most often vex and disappoint them? Who are the first to be led away from what is right, and the last to remember cautions and good advice? Who are the most difficult to keep in order and bounds? Who most frequently break out into open sin, disgrace the name they bear, make their friends unhappy, embitter the old age of their relations, and bring down grey hairs with sorrow to the grave? Depend on it, the answer will generally be, *'The Young Men.'*

Let us ask the magistrates and officers of justice, and mark what they will reply. Who go to public-houses and beer-shops most? Who are the greatest Sabbath-breakers? Who make up riotous mobs and seditious meetings? Who are oftenest taken up for drunkenness, breaches of the peace, fighting, poaching, stealing, assaults, and the like? Who fill the jails, and penitentiaries, and convict ships? Who are the class which requires the most incessant watching and looking after? Depend on it, they will at once point to the same quarter,—they will say, *'The Young Men.'*

Let us turn to the upper classes, and mark the report we shall get from them. In one family the sons are always wasting time, health, and money, in the selfish pursuit of pleasure. In another, the sons will follow no profession, and fritter away the most precious years of their lives in doing nothing. In another, they take up a profession as a mere form, but pay no attention to its duties. In another, they are always forming wrong connections, gambling, getting into debt, associating with bad companions, keeping their friends in a constant fever of anxiety. Alas, rank, title, wealth, and education do not prevent these things! Anxious fathers, heart-broken mothers, and sorrowing sisters could tell sad tales about them, if the truth were known. Many a family, with everything this world can give, numbers among its connections some name that is never named,—or only named with regret and shame,—some son, some brother, some cousin, some nephew,—who will have his own way, and is a grief to all who know him.

There is seldom a rich family, which has not got some thorn in its side, some blot in its page of happiness, some constant source of pain and anxiety;—often, far too often, is not this the true cause, 'The Young Men'?

What shall we say to these things? These are facts,—plain staring facts,—facts which meet us on every side,—facts which cannot be denied. How dreadful this is! How dreadful the thought, that every time I meet a young man, I meet one who is in all probability an enemy of God,—travelling in the broad way, which leads to destruction,—unfit for heaven! Surely, with such facts before me, you will not wonder that I exhort you,—you must allow there is a cause.

(2) For another thing, *death and judgment are before young men, even as others,* and they nearly all seem to forget it.

Young men, it is appointed unto you once to die; and however strong and healthy you may be now, the day of your death is perhaps very near. I see young people sick as well as old. I bury youthful corpses as well as aged. I read the names of persons no older than yourselves in every churchyard. I learn from books that, excepting infancy and old age, more die between thirteen and twenty-three than at any other season of life. And yet you live as if you were sure at present not to die at all.

Are you thinking you will mind these things *tomorrow?* Remember the words of Solomon: 'Boast not thyself of tomorrow; for thou knowest not what a day may bring forth' (Prov. 27:1). 'Serious things tomorrow', said a heathen, to one who warned him of coming danger; but his tomorrow never came.[1] Tomorrow is the devil's day, but today is God's. Satan cares not how spiritual your intentions may be, and how holy your resolutions, if only they are fixed for *tomorrow*. Oh, give not place to the devil in this matter! Answer him, 'No, Satan! It shall be today, today.' All men do not live to be patriarchs, like Isaac and Jacob. Many children die before their fathers. David had to mourn the death of his two finest sons; Job lost all his ten children in one day. Your lot may be like one of theirs, and when death summons, it will be vain to talk of tomorrow,—you must go at once.

Are you thinking you will have a *convenient season* to mind these things by and by? So thought Felix and the Athenians to whom Paul preached; but it never came (Acts 24:10-22; 17:22). Hell is paved with such fancies. Better make sure work while you can. Leave nothing unsettled that is eternal. Run no risk when your soul is at stake. Believe me, the salvation of a soul is no easy matter. All need a 'great' salvation, whether young or old; all need to be born again,—all need to be washed in Christ's blood,—all need to be sanctified by the Spirit. Happy is that man who does not leave these things uncertain, but never rests till he has the witness of the Spirit within him, that he is a child of God.

Young men, your time is short. Your days are but a span long,—a shadow, a vapour,—a tale that is soon told. Your bodies are not brass. 'Even the young men', says Isaiah, 'shall utterly fall' (Isa. 40:30). Your health may be taken from you

---

[1] According to the Greek historian Plutarch, Archias, a general of ancient Thebes, postponed reading a letter which revealed a plot to kill him the following day.

in a moment:—it only needs a fall, a fever, an inflammation, a broken blood vessel,—and the worm would soon feed upon you. There is but a step between any one of you and death. This night your soul might be required of you (Luke 12:20). You are fast going the way of all the earth,—you will soon be gone. Your life is all uncertainty,—your death and judgment are perfectly sure. You too must hear the archangel's trumpet, and go forth to stand before the great white throne (Rev. 20:11),—you too must obey that summons, which Jerome[2] says was always ringing in his ears: 'Arise, ye dead, and come to judgment.' 'Surely I come quickly' (Rev. 22:7), is the language of the Judge himself. I cannot, dare not, will not let you alone.

Oh, that you would all lay to heart the words of the Preacher: 'Rejoice, O young man, in thy youth, and let thy heart cheer thee in the days of thy youth, and walk in the ways of thine heart, and in the sight of thine eyes; but know thou, that for all these things God will bring thee into judgment' (Eccles. 11:9). Wonderful, that with such a prospect, any man can be careless and unconcerned! Surely none are so mad as those who are content to live unprepared to die. Surely the unbelief of men is the most amazing thing in the world. Well may the clearest prophecy in the Bible begin with these words, 'Who hath believed our report?' (Isa. 53:1). Well may the Lord Jesus say, 'When the Son of man cometh, shall he find faith on the earth?' (Luke 18:8). Young men, I fear lest this be the report of many of you in the courts above: 'They will not believe.' I fear

---

[2] Jerome (AD 345–420), an early church father best known for his translation of the Bible into Latin (the Vulgate).

lest you be hurried out of the world, and awake to find out, too late, that death and judgment are realities. I fear all this, and therefore I exhort you.

(3) For another thing, *what young men will be, in all probability depends on what they are now*, and they seem to forget this.

Youth is the seed-time of full age,—the moulding season in the little space of human life,—the turning-point in the history of man's mind.

By the shoot, we judge of the tree,—by the blossoms we judge of the fruit,—by the spring we judge of the harvest,—by the morning we judge of the day,—and by the character of the young man, we may generally judge what he will be when he grows up.

Young men, be not deceived. Think not you can, at will, serve lusts and pleasures in your beginning, and then go and serve God with ease at your latter end. Think not you can live with Esau, and then die with Jacob. It is a mockery to deal with God and your souls in such a fashion. It is an awful mockery to suppose you can give the flower of your strength to the world and the devil, and then put off the King of kings with the scraps and leavings of your hearts,—the wreck and remnant of your powers. It is an awful mockery, and you may find to your cost the thing cannot be done.

I daresay you are reckoning on a *late repentance*. You know not what you are doing. You are reckoning without God.

Repentance and faith are the gifts of God, and gifts that he often withholds, when they have been long offered in vain. I grant you true repentance is never too late, but I warn you at the same time, late repentance is seldom true. I grant you, one penitent thief was converted in his last hours, that no man might despair; but I warn you, only one was converted, that no man might presume. I grant you it is written, Jesus is 'able to save them to the uttermost that come unto God by him' (Heb. 7:25). But I warn you, it is also written by the same Spirit, 'Because I have called, and ye refused, I also will laugh at your calamity; I will mock when your fear cometh' (Prov. 1:24, 26).

Believe me, you will find it no easy matter to turn to God just when you please. It is a true saying of good Archbishop Leighton: 'The way of sin is down hill; a man cannot stop when he would.' Holy desires and serious convictions are not like the servants of the centurion, ready to come and go at your desire (Matt. 8:5); rather are they like the unicorn in Job,—they will not obey your voice, nor attend at your bidding (Job 39:9). It was said of a famous general of old,[3] when he could have taken the city[4] he warred against, he *would not*, and by and by when he would, he *could not*. Beware, lest the same kind of event befall you in the matter of eternal life.

Why do I say all this? I say it because of *the force of habit*. I say it because experience tells me that people's hearts are seldom changed if they are not changed when young. Seldom indeed

---

[3] Hannibal of Carthage (247–c. 181 BC), one of the greatest military commanders in history.

[4] The city of Rome.

are men converted when they are old. Habits have long roots. Sin once allowed to nestle in your bosom, will not be turned out at your bidding. Custom becomes second nature, and its chains are threefold cords not easily broken. Well says the prophet, 'Can the Ethiopian change his skin, or the leopard his spots? then may ye also do good, that are accustomed to do evil' (Jer. 13:23). Habits are like stones rolling down hill,—the further they roll, the faster and more ungovernable is their course. Habits, like trees, are strengthened by age. A boy may bend an oak, when it is a sapling,—a hundred men cannot root it up, when it is a full-grown tree. A child can wade over the Thames at its fountain-head,—the largest ship in the world can float in it when it gets near the sea. So it is with habits: the older the stronger,—the longer they have held possession, the harder they will be to cast out. They grow with our growth, and strengthen with our strength. Custom is the nurse of sin. Every fresh act of sin lessens fear and remorse, hardens our hearts, blunts the edge of our conscience, and increases our evil inclination.

Young men, you may fancy I am laying too much stress on this point. If you had seen old men, as I have done, on the brink of the grave, feelingless, seared, callous, dead, cold, hard as the nether[5] mill-stone,—you would not think so. Believe me, you cannot stand still in the affairs of your souls. Habits of good or evil are daily strengthening in your hearts. Every day you are either getting nearer to God, or further off. Every year that you continue impenitent, the wall of division between

---

[5] The lower mill-stone was the harder of two large circular stones, one placed on top of the other, used for grinding grain in a mill.

you and heaven becomes higher and thicker, and the gulf to be crossed deeper and broader. Oh, dread the hardening effect of constant lingering in sin! Now is the accepted time. See that your flight be not in the winter of your days. If you seek not the Lord when young, the strength of habit is such that you will probably never seek him at all.

I fear this, and therefore I exhort you.

(4) For another thing, *the devil uses special diligence to destroy the souls of young men*, and they seem not to know it.

Satan knows well that you will make up the next generation, and therefore he employs every art betimes to make you his own. I would not have you ignorant of his devices.

You are those on whom he plays off all his choicest temptations. He spreads his net with the most watchful carefulness, to entangle your hearts. He baits his traps with the sweetest morsels, to get you into his power. He displays his wares before your eyes with his utmost ingenuity, in order to make you buy his sugared poisons, and eat his accursed dainties. You are the grand object of his attack. May the Lord rebuke him, and deliver you out of his hands.

Young men, beware of being taken by his snares. He will try to throw dust in your eyes, and prevent you seeing anything in its true colours. He would fain make you think evil good, and good evil (Isa. 5:20). He will paint, and gild, and dress up sin, in order to make you fall in love with it (2 Cor. 11:15). He will deform, and misrepresent, and caricature true religion, in order to make you take a dislike to it. He will exalt the pleasures of wickedness,—but he will hide from you the sting. He will lift up before your eyes the cross and its painfulness,—but he will keep out of sight the eternal crown. He will promise you everything, as he did to Christ, if you will only serve him (Matt. 4:8). He will even help you to wear a form of religion, if you will only neglect the power (2 Tim. 3:5). He will tell you at the beginning of your lives, it is *too soon* to serve God,—he will tell you at the end, it is *too late*. Oh, be not deceived!

You little know the danger you are in from this enemy; and it is this very ignorance which makes me afraid. You are like blind men, walking amidst holes and pitfalls; you do not see the perils which are around you on every side (Luke 6:39).

Your enemy is *mighty*. He is called 'the prince of this world' (John 14:30). He opposed our Lord Jesus Christ all through his ministry. He tempted Adam and Eve to eat the forbidden fruit, and so brought sin and death into the world (Gen. 3). He tempted even David, the man after God's own heart, and caused his latter days to be full of sorrow (2 Sam. 11:2). He tempted even Peter, the chosen apostle, and made him deny his Lord (Matt. 26:69). Surely his enmity is not to be despised?

Your enemy is *restless*. He never sleeps. He is always going about as a roaring lion, seeking whom he may devour (1 Pet. 5:8). He is ever going to and fro in the earth, and walking up and down in it (Job 1:7). You may be careless about your souls: he is not. He wants them to make them miserable, like himself, and will have them if he can. Surely his enmity is not to be despised?

And your enemy is *cunning*. For near six thousand years

he has been reading one book, and that book is the heart of man. He ought to know it well, and he does know it;—all its weakness, all its deceitfulness, all its folly. And he has a store of temptations such as are most likely to do it harm. Never will you go to the place where he will not find you. Go into towns,—he will be there. Go into a wilderness,—he will be there also. Sit among drunkards and revellers,—and he will be there to help you. Listen to preaching,—and he will be there to distract you. Surely such enmity is not to be despised?

Young men, this enemy is working hard for your destruction, however little you may think it. You are the prize for which he is specially contending. He foresees you must either be the blessings or the curses of your day, and he is trying hard to effect a lodgement[6] in your hearts thus early, in order that you may help forward his kingdom by and by. Well does he understand that to spoil the bud is the surest way to mar the flower.

Oh that your eyes were opened, like those of Elisha's servant in Dothan (2 Kings 6:13-17)! Oh that you did but see what Satan is scheming against your peace! I must warn you,—I must exhort you. Whether you will hear or not, I cannot, dare not, leave you alone.

(5) For another thing, *young men need exhorting, because of the sorrow it will save them, to begin serving God now.*

Sin is the mother of all sorrow, and no sort of sin appears to give a man so much misery and pain as the sins of his youth.

---

[6] Lodgement: a place in which a person or thing is located; a dwelling.

The foolish acts he did,—the time he wasted,—the mistakes he made,—the bad company he kept,—the harm he did himself, both body and soul,—the chances of happiness he threw away,—the openings of usefulness he neglected;—all these are things that often embitter the conscience of an old man, throw a gloom on the evening of his days, and fill the later hours of his life with self-reproach and shame.

Some men could tell you of the untimely *loss of health*, brought on by youthful sins. Disease racks their limbs with pain, and life is almost a weariness. Their muscular strength is so wasted, that a grasshopper seems a burden. Their eye has become prematurely dim, and their natural force abated. The sun of their health has gone down while it is yet day, and they mourn to see their flesh and body consumed. Believe me, this is a bitter cup to drink.

Others could give you sad accounts of the *consequences of idleness*. They threw away the golden opportunity for learning. They would not get wisdom at the time when their minds were most able to receive it, and their memories most ready to retain it. And now it is too late. They have not leisure to sit down and learn. They have no longer the same power, even if they had the leisure. Lost time can never be redeemed. This too is a bitter cup to drink.

Others could tell you of grievous *mistakes in judgment*, from which they suffer all their lives long. They would have their own way. They would not take advice. They formed some connection which has been altogether ruinous to their happiness.

They chose a profession for which they were entirely unsuited. And they see it all now. But their eyes are only open when the mistake cannot be retrieved. Oh, this is also a bitter cup to drink!

Young men, young men, I wish you did but know the comfort of a conscience not burdened with a long list of youthful sins. These are the wounds that pierce the deepest. These are the arrows that drink up a man's spirit. This is the iron that enters into the soul. Be merciful to yourselves. Seek the Lord early, and so you will be spared many a bitter tear.

This is the truth that Job seems to have felt. He says, 'Thou writest bitter things against me, and makest me to possess the iniquities of my youth' (Job 13:26). So also his friend Zophar, speaking of the wicked, says, 'His bones are full of the sins of his youth, which shall lie down with him in the dust' (Job 20:11).

David also seems to have felt it. He says to the Lord, 'Remember not the sins of my youth, nor my transgressions' (Psa. 25:7).

Beza, the great Swiss Reformer, felt it so strongly, that he named it in his will as a special mercy that he had been called out from the world, by the grace of God, at the age of sixteen.

Go and ask believers now, and I think many an one will tell you much the same. 'Oh that I could live my young days over again!' he will most probably say. 'Oh that I had spent the beginning of my life in a better fashion! Oh that I had not laid the foundation of evil habits so strongly in the spring-time of my course!'

Young men, I want to save you all this sorrow, if I can. Hell itself is truth known too late. Be wise in time. What youth sows, old age must reap. Give not the most precious season of your life to that which will not comfort you in your latter end. Sow to yourselves rather in righteousness: break up your fallow ground, sow not among thorns.

Sin may go lightly from your hand, or run smoothly off your tongue now, but depend on it, sin and you will meet again by and by, however little you may like it. Old wounds will often ache and give pain long after they are healed, and only a scar remains:—so may you find it with your sins. The footprints of animals have been found on the surface of rocks that were once wet sand, thousands of years after the animal that made them has perished and passed away;—so also it may be with your sins.

'Experience', says the proverb, 'keeps a dear school, but fools will learn in no other.' I want you all to escape the misery of learning in that school. I want you to avoid the wretchedness that youthful sins are sure to entail. This is the last reason why I exhort you.

Part Two

Special Dangers to Young Men

2. In the second place, *There are some special dangers against which young men need to be warned.*

(1) One danger to young men is *pride.*

I know well that all souls are in fearful peril. Old or young, it matters not; all have a race to run, a battle to fight, a heart to mortify, a world to overcome, a body to keep under, a devil to resist; and we may well say, Who is sufficient for these things? But still every age and condition has its own peculiar snares and temptations, and it is well to know them. He that is forewarned is forearmed. If I can only persuade you to be on your guard against the dangers I am going to name, I am sure I shall do your souls an essential service.

Pride is the oldest sin in the world. Indeed, it was before the world. Satan and his angels fell by pride. They were not satisfied with their first estate. Thus, pride stocked hell with its first inhabitants.

Pride cast Adam out of paradise. He was not content with the place God assigned him. He tried to raise himself, and fell. Thus sin, sorrow, and death entered in by pride.

Pride sits in all our hearts by nature. We are born proud. Pride makes us rest satisfied with ourselves,—think we are good enough as we are,—stop our ears against advice,—refuse the gospel of Christ,—turn every one to his own way. But pride never reigns anywhere so powerfully as in the heart of a young man.

How common is it to see young men heady, high-minded, and impatient of counsel! How often they are rude and discourteous to all about them, thinking they are not valued and honoured as they deserve! How often they will not stop to listen to a hint from an older person! They think they know everything. They are full of conceit of their own wisdom. They reckon elderly people, and especially their relations, stupid, dull, and slow. They fancy they want no teaching or instruction themselves: they understand all things. It makes them almost angry to be spoken to. Like young horses, they cannot bear the least control. They must needs be independent, and have their own way. They seem to think, like those whom Job mentioned, 'We are the people, and wisdom shall die with us' (Job 12:2). And this is all pride.

Such an one was Rehoboam, who despised the counsel of the old experienced men who stood before his father, and hearkened to the advice of the young men of his own generation. He lived to reap the consequences of his folly. There are many like him.

Such an one was the prodigal son in the parable, who must needs have the portion of goods which fell to him, and set up for himself. He could not submit to live quietly under his father's roof, but would go into a far country, and be his own master. Like the little child that will leave its mother's hand and walk alone, he soon smarted for his folly. He became wiser when he had to eat husks with the swine. But there are many like him.

Young men, I beseech you earnestly, beware of pride. Two things are said to be very rare sights in the world,—one is a young man humble, and the other is an old man content. I fear this saying is only too true.

Be not proud of your own abilities,—your own strength,—your own knowledge,—your own appearance,—your own cleverness. Be not proud of yourself, and your endowments of any kind. It all comes from not knowing yourself and the world. The older you grow, and the more you see, the less reason you will find for being proud. Ignorance and inexperience are the pedestal of pride; once let the pedestal be removed, and pride will soon come down.

Remember how often Scripture sets before us the excellence of a humble spirit. How strongly we are warned 'not to think of ourselves more highly than we ought to think' (Rom. 12:3)! How plainly we are told, 'If any man think that he knoweth anything, he knoweth nothing yet as he ought to know' (1 Cor. 8:2)! How strict is the command, 'Put on humbleness of mind' (Col. 3:12)! And again, 'Be clothed with humility' (1 Pet. 5:5). Alas, this is a garment of which many seem not to have so much as a rag.

Think of the great example our Lord Jesus Christ leaves us in this respect. He washed the feet of his disciples, saying, 'Ye should do as I have done to you' (John 13:15). It is written, 'Though he was rich, yet for your sakes he became poor' (2 Cor. 8:9). And again, He 'made himself of no reputation, and took upon him the form of a servant, and was made in the likeness of men; and being found in fashion as a man, he humbled himself' (Phil. 2:7, 8). Surely to be proud is to be more like the devil and fallen Adam, than like Christ. Surely, it can never be mean[7] and low-spirited to be like him.

Think of the wisest man that ever lived—I mean Solomon. See how he speaks of himself as a 'little child', as one who 'knew not how to go out or come in', or manage for himself (1 Kings 3:7, 8). That was a very different spirit from his brother Absalom's, who thought himself equal to anything: 'Oh that I were made judge in the land, that every man which hath any suit or cause might come unto me, and I would do him justice!' (2 Sam. 15:4). That was a very different spirit from his brother Adonijah's, who 'exalted himself, saying, I will be king' (1 Kings 1:5). Humility was the beginning of Solomon's wisdom. He writes it down as his own experience, 'Seest thou a man wise in his own conceit? There is more hope of a fool than of him' (Prov. 26:12).

Young men, lay to heart the Scriptures here quoted. Do not be too confident in your own judgment. Cease to be sure that you are always right, and others wrong. Be distrustful of your own opinion, when you find it contrary to that of older men than yourselves, and specially to that of your own parents. Age

---

[7] Mean: unkind, spiteful, unfair.

gives experience, and therefore deserves respect. It is a mark of Elihu's wisdom, in the book of Job, that he waited till Job had spoken, because they were older than himself (Job 32:4). And afterwards he said, 'I am young, and ye are very old; wherefore I was afraid, and durst not show you mine opinion. I said, Days should speak, and multitude of years should teach wisdom' (Job 32:6, 7). Modesty and silence are beautiful graces in young people. Never be ashamed of being a learner: Jesus was one at twelve years; when he was found in the temple, he was 'sitting in the midst of the doctors, both hearing them, and asking them questions' (Luke 2:46). The wisest men would tell you they are always learners, and are humbled to find after all how little they know. The great Sir Isaac Newton[8] used to say that he felt himself no better than a little child who had picked up a few precious stones on the shore of the sea of knowledge.

Young men, if you would be wise, if you would be happy, remember the warning I give you,—Beware of pride.

(2) Another danger to young men is *the love of pleasure*.

Youth is the time when our passions are strongest,—and like unruly children, cry most loudly for indulgence. Youth is the time when we have generally most health and strength: death seems far away, and to enjoy ourselves in this life seems everything. Youth is the time when most people have few earthly cares or anxieties to take up their attention. And all these things help to make young men think of nothing so much as pleasure. 'I

[8] Sir Isaac Newton (1642–1727), English physicist and mathematician.

serve lusts and pleasures': that is the true answer many a young man should give, if asked, 'Whose servant are you?'

Young men, time would fail me if I were to tell you all the fruits this love of pleasure produces, and all the ways in which it may do you harm. Why should I speak of revelling, feasting, drinking, gambling, theatre-going, dancing, and the like? Few are to be found who do not know something of these things by bitter experience. And these are only instances. All things that give a feeling of excitement for the time,—all things that drown thought, and keep the mind in a constant whirl,—all things that please the senses and gratify the flesh;—these are the sort of things that have mighty power at your time of life, and they owe their power to the love of pleasure. Be on your guard. Be not like those of whom Paul speaks, 'Lovers of pleasures more than lovers of God' (2 Tim. 3:4).

Remember what I say: if you would cleave to earthly pleasures,—these are the things which *murder souls*. There is no surer way to get a seared conscience and a hard impenitent heart than to give way to the desires of the flesh and mind. It seems nothing at first, but it tells in the long run.

Consider what Peter says: 'Abstain from fleshly lusts, which war against the soul' (1 Pet. 2:11). They destroy the soul's peace, break down its strength, lead it into hard captivity, and make it a slave.

Consider what Paul says: 'Mortify your members which are upon the earth' (Col. 3:5). 'They that are Christ's have crucified the flesh with its affections and lusts' (Gal. 5:24). 'I keep under my body, and bring it into subjection' (1 Cor. 9:27). Once the body was a perfect mansion of the soul;—now it is all corrupt and disordered, and needs constant watching. It is a burden to the soul,—not a helpmeet; a hindrance,—not an assistance. It may become a useful servant, but it is always a bad master.

Consider again the words of Paul: 'Put ye on the Lord Jesus Christ, and make not provision for the flesh, to fulfil the lusts thereof' (Rom. 13:14). 'These', says Leighton,[9] 'are the words, the very reading of which so wrought with Augustine,[10] that from a licentious young man he turned a faithful servant of Jesus Christ.' Young men, I wish this might be the case with all of you.

Remember, again, if you will cleave to earthly pleasures, they are all *unsatisfying, empty, and vain*. Like the locusts of the vision in Revelation, they seem to have crowns on their heads: but like the same locusts, you will find they have stings,—real stings,—in their tails. All is not gold that glitters. All is not good that tastes sweet. All is not real pleasure that pleases for a time.

Go and take your fill of earthly pleasures if you will,—you will never find your heart satisfied with them. There will always be a voice within, crying, like the horse-leech in the Proverbs, 'Give, give!' (Prov. 30:15). There is an empty place there, which nothing but God can fill. You will find, as Solomon did by experience, that earthly pleasures are but a vain show,—vanity and vexation of spirit,—whited sepulchres, fair to look at

---

[9] Robert Leighton (1611–84), Archbishop of Glasgow.

[10] Augustine of Hippo (AD 354–430), early church father and theologian whose writings greatly influenced Western Christianity and philosophy. His conversion from a life of immorality is well told in *Confessions*, perhaps his most famous work.

without, full of ashes and corruption within. Better be wise in time. Better write 'poison' on all earthly pleasures. The most lawful of them must be used with moderation. All of them are soul-destroying if you give them your heart.[11]

And here I will not shrink from warning all young men to remember the seventh commandment (Exod. 20:14); to beware of adultery and fornication, of all impurity of every kind. I fear there is often a want of plain speaking on this part of God's law. But when I see how prophets and apostles have dealt with this subject,—when I observe the open way in which the Reformers of our own church denounce it,—when I see the number of young men who walk in the footsteps of Reuben, and Hophni, and Phinehas, and Amnon,—I for one cannot, with a good conscience, hold my peace. I doubt whether the world is any better for the excessive silence which prevails upon this commandment. For my own part, I feel it would be false and unscriptural delicacy, in addressing young men, not to speak of that which is pre-eminently *the young man's sin*.

The breach of the seventh commandment is the sin above all others, that, as Hosea says, 'takes away the heart' (Hos. 4:11). It is the sin that leaves deeper scars upon the soul than any sin that a man can commit. It is a sin that slays its thousands in every age, and has overthrown not a few of the saints of God in time past. Lot, and Samson, and David are fearful proofs. It is the sin that man dares to smile at, and smooths over under the names of *gaiety, unsteadiness, wildness,* and *irregularity.* But

[11] 'Pleasure', says Adams on Second Peter, 'must first have the *warrant*, that it be without sin;—then the *measure*, that it be without excess.'

it is the sin that the devil peculiarly rejoices over, for he is the 'unclean spirit'; and it is the sin that God peculiarly abhors, and declares he 'will judge' (Heb. 13:4).

Young men, 'flee fornication' (1 Cor. 6:18) if you love life. 'Let no man deceive you with vain words: for because of these things cometh the wrath of God upon the children of disobedience' (Eph. 5:6). Flee the *occasions* of it,—the company of those who might draw you into it,—the places where you might be tempted to it. Read what our Lord says about it in Matthew 5:28. Be like holy Job: Make 'a covenant with your eyes' (Job 31:1). Flee *talking* of it. It is one of the things that ought not so much as to be named. You cannot handle pitch[12] and not be defiled. Flee the *thoughts* of it; resist them, mortify them, pray against them,—make any sacrifice rather than give way. Imagination is the hotbed where this sin is too often hatched. Guard your thoughts, and there is little fear about your deeds.

Consider the caution I have been giving. If you forget all else, do not let this be forgotten.

(3) Another danger to young men is *thoughtlessness and inconsideration*.

Want of thought is one simple reason why thousands of souls are cast away for ever. Men will not consider,—will not look forward,—will not look around them,—will not reflect on the end of their present course, and the sure consequences of their

---

[12] Pitch: a black sticky substance derived from coal tar and traditionally used to caulk or waterproof the seams of wooden sailing vessels.

present ways,—and awake at last to find they are damned for want of thinking.

Young men, none are in more danger of this than yourselves. You know little of the perils around you, and so you are heedless how you walk. You hate the trouble of sober, quiet thinking, and so you form wrong decisions and run your heads into sorrow. Young Esau must needs have his brother's pottage and sell his birthright: he never *thought* how much he should one day want it. Young Simeon and Levi must needs avenge their sister Dinah, and slay the Shechemites; they never *considered* how much trouble and anxiety they might bring on their father Jacob and his house. Job seems to have been specially afraid of this thoughtlessness among his children: it is written, that when they had a feast, and 'the days of their feasting were gone about, Job sent and sanctified them, and rose up early in the morning and offered burnt offerings, according to the number of them all: for Job said, It may be that my sons have sinned, and cursed God in their hearts. Thus did Job continually' (Job 1:5).

Believe me, this world is not a world in which we can do well without thinking, and least of all do well in the matter of our souls. 'Don't think', whispers Satan: he knows that an unconverted heart is like a dishonest tradesman's books, it will not bear close inspection. 'Consider your ways', says the word of God,—stop and think,—consider and be wise. Well says the Spanish proverb, 'Hurry comes from the devil.' Just as men marry in haste and then repent at leisure, so they make mistakes about their souls in a minute, and then suffer for it for years.

Just as a bad servant does wrong, and then says, 'I never gave it a thought', so young men run into sin, and then say, 'I did not think about it,—it did not look like sin.' Not look like sin! What would you have? Sin will not come to you, saying, 'I am sin'; it would do little harm if it did. Sin always seems 'good, and pleasant, and desirable', at the time of commission (Gen. 3:6). Oh, get wisdom, get discretion! Remember the words of Solomon: 'Ponder the paths of thy feet, and let all thy ways be established' (Prov. 4:26). It is a wise saying of Lord Bacon, 'Do nothing rashly. Stay a little, that you make an end the sooner.'

Some, I dare say, will object that I am asking what is unreasonable; that youth is not the time of life when people ought to be grave and thoughtful. I answer, there is little danger of their being too much so in the present day. Foolish talking, and jesting, and joking, and excessive merriment, are only too common. Doubtless there is a time for all things; but to be always light and trifling is anything but wise. What says the wisest of men?—'It is better to go to the house of mourning than to go to the house of feasting: for that is the end of all men; and the living will lay it to his heart. Sorrow is better than laughter: for by the sadness of the countenance the heart is made better. The heart of the wise is in the house of mourning; but the heart of fools is in the house of mirth' (Eccles. 7:2-4). Matthew Henry[13] tells a story of a great statesman[14] in Queen Elizabeth's time, who retired from public life in his latter days, and gave himself up to serious

---

[13] Matthew Henry (1662–1714), Puritan minister whose popular commentary on the Bible has been of immense help to Christians for more than 300 years.

[14] Francis Walsingham (c. 1532–90), Elizabeth I's Secretary of State and Spymaster.

thought. His former carefree companions came to visit him, and told him he was becoming melancholy: 'No', he replied, 'I am *serious*; for all are serious round about me. God is serious in observing us,—Christ is serious in interceding for us,—the Spirit is serious in striving with us,—the truths of God are serious,—our spiritual enemies are serious in their endeavours to ruin us,—poor lost sinners are serious in hell;—and why then should not you and I be serious too?'

Oh, young men, learn to be thoughtful! Learn to consider what you are doing, and whither you are going. Make time for calm reflection. Commune with your own heart, and be still. Remember my caution:—Do not be lost merely for the want of thought.

(4) Another danger to young men is *contempt of religion*.

This also is one of your special dangers. I always observe that none pay so little outward respect to religion as young men. None attend so badly on the means of grace,[15]—none take so little part in our services, when they are present at them,—use Bibles and Prayer Books so little,—sing so little,—listen to preaching so little. None are so generally absent at prayer-meetings, and lectures, and all such week-day helps to the soul. Young men seem to think they do not need these things,—they may be good for women and old men, but not for them. They

[15] The means of grace are the instruments God uses to convert and bless his people. They include such things as the reading and preaching of the word of God, prayer, singing of psalms, hymns and spiritual songs, the fellowship of saints, and the sacraments of baptism and the Lord's supper.

appear ashamed of seeming to care about their souls: one would almost fancy they reckoned it a disgrace to go to heaven at all. And this is *contempt of religion*;—it is the same spirit which made the young people of Bethel mock Elisha;—and of this spirit I say to all young men, Beware! If it be worth while to have a religion, it is worth while to be in earnest about it.

Contempt of holy things is the high road to infidelity. Once let a man begin to make a jest and joke of any part of Christianity, and I am never surprised to hear that he has turned out a downright unbeliever.

Young men, have you really made up your minds to this? Have you fairly looked into the gulf which is before you, if you persist in despising religion? Call to mind the words of David: 'The fool hath said in his heart, There is no God' (Psa. 14:1). The *fool*, and none but the fool!—He has *said* it: but he has never proved it! Remember, if ever there was a book which has been proved true from beginning to end, by every kind of evidence, that book is the Bible. It has defied the attacks of all enemies and fault-finders. 'The word of the Lord is indeed *tried*' (Psa. 18:30). It has been tried in every way, and the more it has been tried, the more evidently has it been shown to be the very handiwork of God himself. What will you believe, if you do not believe the Bible? There is no choice but to believe something ridiculous and absurd. Depend on it, no man is so grossly credulous as the man who denies the Bible to be the word of God;—and if it be the word of God, take heed that you despise it not.

Men may tell you there are difficulties in the Bible;—things hard to be understood. It would not be God's book if there were not. And what if there are? You do not despise medicines because you cannot explain all that your doctor does by them. But whatever men may say, the things needful to salvation are as clear as daylight. Be very sure of this,—people never reject the Bible because they cannot understand it. They understand it only too well; they understand that it condemns their own behaviour; they understand that it witnesses against their own sins, and summons them to judgment. They try to believe it is false and useless, because they do not like to allow it is true. 'A bad life', said the celebrated Lord Rochester,[16] laying his hand on the Bible, 'a bad life is the only grand objection to this book.' 'Men question the truth of Christianity', says South,[17] 'because they hate the practice of it.'

Young men, when did God ever fail to keep his word? Never. What he has said, he has always done; and what he has spoken, he has always made good. Did he fail to keep his word at the flood?—No. Did he fail with Sodom and Gomorrha?—No. Did he fail with unbelieving Jerusalem?—No. Has he failed with the Jews up to this very hour?—No. He has never failed to fulfil his word. Take care, lest you be found amongst those by whom God's word is despised.

[16] John Wilmot, 2nd Earl of Rochester (1647–80), English poet and courtier of King Charles II's Restoration court. Rochester was the embodiment of that new licentious, anti-Puritan era, and he was as well known for his immoral lifestyle as for his poetry. He died at the age of 33 from a sexually transmitted disease.

[17] Robert South (1634–1716), English episcopal churchman who was known for his combative preaching.

Never laugh at religion. Never make a jest of sacred things. Never mock those who are serious and in earnest about their souls. The time may come when you will count those happy whom you laughed at,—a time when your laughter will be turned into sorrow, and your mockery into heaviness.

(5) Another danger to young men is *the fear of man's opinion.*

'The fear of man' does indeed 'bringeth a snare' (Prov. 29:25). It is terrible to observe the power which it has over most minds, and especially over the minds of the young. Few seem to have any opinions of their own, or to think for themselves. Like dead fish, they go with the stream and tide: what others think right, they think right; and what others call wrong, they call wrong too. There are not many original thinkers in the world. Most men are like sheep, they follow a leader. If it was the fashion of the day to be Romanists, they would be Romanists,—if to be Mahometans they would be Mahometans. They dread the idea of going against the current of the times. In a word, the opinion of the day becomes their religion, their creed, their Bible, and their God.

The thought, 'What will my friends say or think of me?' nips many a good inclination in the bud. The fear of being observed upon, laughed at, or ridiculed, prevents many a good habit being taken up. There are Bibles that would be read this very day, if the owners dared. They know they ought to read them, but they are afraid:—'What will people say?' There are knees that would be bent in prayer this very night, but the fear of man forbids it:—'What would my wife, my brother, my friend, my companion say, if they saw me praying?' Alas, what wretched slavery this is, and yet how common! 'I feared the people', said Saul to Samuel: and so he transgressed the commandment of the Lord (1 Sam. 15:24). 'I am afraid of the Jews', said Zedekiah, the graceless king of Judah: and so he disobeyed the advice which Jeremiah gave him (Jer. 38:19). Herod was afraid of what his guests would think of him: so he did that which made him 'exceeding sorry',—he beheaded John the Baptist. Pilate feared offending the Jews: so he did that which he knew in his conscience was unjust,—he delivered up Jesus to be crucified. If this be not slavery, what is?

Young men, I want you all to be free from this bondage. I want you each to care nothing for man's opinion, when the path of duty is clear. Believe me, it is a great thing to be able to say 'No!' Here was good King Jehoshaphat's weak point,—he was too easy and yielding in his dealings with Ahab, and hence many of his troubles (1 Kings 22:4). Learn to say 'No!' Let not the fear of not seeming good-natured make you unable to do it. When sinners entice you, be able to say decidedly, 'I will not consent' (Prov. 1:10).

Consider only how *unreasonable* this fear of man is. How short-lived is man's enmity, and how little harm he can do you! 'Who art thou, that thou shouldest be afraid of a man that shall die, and of the son of man, which shall be made as grass: and forgettest the LORD thy maker, that hath stretched forth the heavens, and laid the foundations of the earth?' (Isa. 51:12, 13).

And how *thankless* is this fear! None will really think better of you for it. The world always respects those most who act boldly for God. Oh, break these bonds, and cast these chains from you! Never be ashamed of letting men see you want to go to heaven. Think it no disgrace to show yourself a servant of God. Never be afraid of doing what is right.

Remember the words of the Lord Jesus: 'Fear not them which kill the body, but are not able to kill the soul: but rather fear him which is able to destroy both soul and body in hell' (Matt. 10:28). Only try to please God, and he can soon make others pleased with you. 'When a man's ways please the LORD, he maketh even his enemies to be at peace with him' (Prov. 16:7).

Young men, be of good courage.—Care not for what the world says or thinks: you will not be with the world always. Can man save your soul?—No. Will man be your judge in the great and dreadful day of account?—No. Can man give you a good conscience in life, a good hope in death, a good answer in the morning of resurrection?—No! no! no! Man can do nothing of the sort. Then 'fear ye not the reproach of men, neither be ye afraid of their revilings: for the moth shall eat them up like a garment, and the worm shall eat them like wool' (Isa. 51:7, 8). Call to mind the saying of good Colonel Gardiner:[18] 'I fear God, and therefore I have none else to fear.' Go and be like him.

Such are the warnings I give you. Lay them to heart. They are worth thinking over. I am much mistaken if they are not greatly needed. The Lord grant they may not have been given you in vain.

[18] Col. James Gardiner (1688–1745), Scottish soldier who fought in the British Army.

Part Three

General Counsels to Young Men

3. In the third place, *I wish to give some general counsels to young men*.

(1) For one thing, *try to get a clear view of the evil of sin*.

Young men, if you did but know what sin is, and what sin has done, you would not think it strange that I exhort you as I do. You do not see it in its true colours. Your eyes are naturally blind to its guilt and danger, and hence you cannot understand what makes me so anxious about you. Oh, let not the devil succeed in persuading you that sin is a small matter!

Think for a moment *what the Bible says about sin*;—how it dwells naturally in the heart of every man and woman alive (Eccles. 7:20; Rom. 3:23),—how it defiles our thoughts, words, and actions, and that continually (Gen. 6:5; Matt. 15:19),—how it renders us all guilty and abominable in the sight of a holy God (Isa. 64:6; Hab. 1:13),—how it leaves us utterly without hope of salvation, if we look to ourselves (Psa. 143:2; Rom. 3:20),—how its fruit in this world is shame, and its wages in the world to come, death (Rom. 6:21, 23). Think calmly of all this. I tell you this day, it is not more sad to be dying of consumption, and not to know it, than it is to be a living man, and not know it.

Think *what an awful change sin has worked* on all our natures. Man is no longer what he was when God formed him out of the dust of the ground. He came out of God's hand upright and sinless (Eccles. 7:29). In the day of his creation he was, like everything else, 'very good' (Gen. 1:31). And what is man now?—A fallen creature, a ruin, a being that shows the marks of corruption all over,—his heart like Nebuchadnezzar, degraded and earthly, looking down and not up,—his affections like a household in disorder, calling no man master, all extravagance and confusion,—his understanding like a lamp flickering in the socket, impotent to guide him, not knowing good from evil,—his will like a rudderless ship, tossed to and fro by every desire, and constant only in choosing any way rather than God's. Alas, what a wreck is man, compared to what he might have been! Well may we understand such figures being used as blindness, deafness, disease, sleep, death, when the Spirit has to give us a picture of man as he is. And man as he is, remember, was so made by sin.

Think, too, *what it has cost to make atonement for sin*, and to provide a pardon and forgiveness for sinners. God's own Son must come into the world, and take upon him our nature, in order to pay the price of our redemption, and deliver us from the curse of a broken law. He who was in the beginning with the Father, and by whom all things were made, must suffer for sin the just for the unjust,—must die the death of a malefactor, before the way to heaven can be laid open to any soul. See the Lord Jesus Christ despised and rejected of men, scourged, mocked, and insulted;—behold him bleeding on the cross of Calvary;—hear him crying in agony, 'My God, my God, why hast thou forsaken me?'—mark how the sun was darkened, and the rocks rent at the sight;—and then consider, young men, what must be the evil and guilt of sin.

Think, also, *what sin has done* already upon the earth. Think how it cast Adam and Eve out of Eden,—brought the flood upon the old world,—caused fire to come down on Sodom and Gomorrha,—drowned Pharaoh and his host in the Red Sea,—destroyed the seven wicked nations of Canaan,—scattered the twelve tribes of Israel over the face of the globe. Sin alone did all this.

Think, moreover, of all the *misery and sorrow that sin has caused*, and is causing at this very day. Pain, disease, and death,—strifes, quarrels, and divisions,—envy, jealousy, and malice,—deceit, fraud, and cheating,—violence, oppression, and robbery,—selfishness, unkindness, and ingratitude; —all these are the fruits of sin. Sin is the parent of them all. Sin it is that has so marred and spoiled the face of God's creation.

Young men, consider these things, and you will not wonder that we preach as we do. Surely, if you did but think of them, you would break with sin for ever. Will you play with poison? Will you sport with hell? Will you take fire in your hand? Will you harbour your deadliest enemy in your bosom? Will you go on living as if it mattered nothing whether your own sins were forgiven or not,—whether sin had dominion over you, or you over sin? Oh, awake to a sense of sin's sinfulness and danger! Remember the words of Solomon: 'Fools,' none but fools, 'make a mock at sin' (Prov. 14:9).

Hear, then, the request that I make of you this day,—pray that God would teach you the real evil of sin. As you would have your soul saved, arise and pray.

(2) For another thing, *seek to become acquainted with our Lord Jesus Christ.*

This is, indeed, the principal thing in religion. This is the corner-stone of Christianity. Until you know this, my warnings and advice will be useless, and your endeavours, whatever they may be, will be in vain. A watch without a mainspring is not more unserviceable than is religion without Christ.

But let me not be misunderstood. It is not the mere knowing Christ's name that I mean,—it is the knowing his mercy, grace, and power,—the knowing him not by the hearing of the ear, but by the experience of your hearts. I want you to know him by faith,—I want you, as Paul says, to know 'the power of his resurrection ... being made conformable unto his death' (Phil. 3:10). I want you to be able to say of him, He is my peace and my strength, my life and my consolation, my Physician and my Shepherd, my Saviour and my God.

Why do I make such a point of this? I do it because in Christ alone 'all fulness dwells' (Col. 1:19),—because in him alone there is full supply of all that we require for the necessities of our souls. Of ourselves we are all poor, empty creatures,—empty of righteousness and peace,—empty of strength and comfort,—empty of courage and patience,—empty of power to stand, or go on, or make progress in this evil world. It is in Christ alone that all these things are to be found,—grace, peace, wisdom, righteousness, sanctification, and redemption. It is just in proportion as we live upon him, that we are strong Christians. It is only when self is nothing and Christ is all our confidence, it is then only that we shall do great exploits. Then only are we armed for the battle of life, and shall overcome. Then only are we prepared for the journey of life, and shall get forward. To live on Christ,—to draw all from Christ,—to do all in the strength of Christ,—to be ever looking unto Christ;—this is the true secret of spiritual prosperity. 'I can do all things', says Paul, 'through Christ which strengtheneth me' (Phil. 4:13).

Young men, I set before you Jesus Christ this day, as the *treasury of your souls*; and I invite you to begin by going to him, if you would so run as to obtain. Let this be your first step,—go to Christ. Do you want to consult friends?—He is the best friend: 'a friend that sticketh closer than a brother' (Prov. 18:24). Do you feel unworthy because of your sins?—Fear not: his blood cleanseth from all sin. He says, 'Though your sins be as scarlet, they shall be as white as snow: though they be red like crimson, they shall be as wool' (Isa. 1:18). Do you feel weak, and unable to follow him?—Fear not: he will give you power to become sons of God. He will give you the Holy Ghost to dwell in you, and seal you for his own; a new heart will he give you, and a new spirit will he put within you. Are you troubled or beset with peculiar infirmities?—Fear not: there is no evil spirit that Jesus cannot cast out,—there is no disease of soul that he cannot heal. Do you feel doubts and fears?—Cast them aside: 'Come unto me', he says (Matt. 11:28); 'him that cometh I will in no wise cast out' (John 6:37). He knows well the heart of a young man. He knows your trials and your temptations, your difficulties and your foes. In the days of his flesh, he was like yourselves,—a young man at Nazareth. He knows by experience a young man's mind. He can be touched with the feeling of your infirmities,—for he suffered himself, being tempted (Heb. 2:18; 4:15). Surely, you will be without excuse if you turn away from such a Saviour and Friend as this.

Hear the request I make of you this day,—if you love life, seek to become acquainted with Jesus Christ.

(3) For another thing, *never forget that nothing is so important as your soul.*

Your soul is eternal. It will live for ever. The world and all that it contains shall pass away,—firm, solid, beautiful, well-ordered as it is, the world shall come to an end. 'The earth also and the works that are therein shall be burned up' (2 Pet. 3:10). The works of statesmen, writers, painters, architects, are all short-lived: your soul will outlive them all. The angel's voice shall proclaim one day that, 'Time shall be no longer' (Rev. 10:6).—But that shall never be said of your souls.

Try, I beseech you, to realize the fact that your soul is the one thing worth living for. It is the part of you which ought always to be first considered. No place, no employment is good for you, which injures your soul. No friend, no companion deserves your confidence, who makes light of your soul's concerns. The man who hurts your person, your property, your character, does you but temporary harm. He is the true enemy who contrives to damage your soul.

Think for a moment what you were sent into the world for. Not merely to eat and drink, and indulge the desires of the flesh,—not merely to dress out your body, and follow its lusts whithersoever they may lead you,—not merely to work, and sleep, and laugh, and talk, and enjoy yourselves, and think of nothing but time. No! you were meant for something higher and better than this. You were placed here to train for eternity. Your body was only intended to be a house for your immortal spirit. It is flying in the face of God's purposes to do as many do,—to make the soul a servant to the body, and not the body a servant to the soul.[19]

Young men, God is no respecter of persons. He regards no man's coat, or purse, or rank, or position. He sees not with man's eyes. The poorest saint that ever died in a workhouse is nobler in his sight than the richest sinner that ever died in a palace. God does not look at riches, titles, learning, beauty, or anything of the kind. One thing only God does look at, and that is the immortal soul. He measures all men by one standard, one measure, one test, one criterion, and that is *the state of their souls*.

---

[19] The Assembly's *Larger Catechism* begins with this admirable question and answer: 'What is the chief and highest end of man? To glorify God, and fully to enjoy him for ever.'

Do not forget this. Keep in view morning, noon, and night, the interests of your soul. Rise up each day desiring that it may prosper,—lie down each evening inquiring of yourself whether it has really got on. Remember Zeuxis, the great painter of old.[20] When men asked him why he laboured so intensely, and took such extreme pains with every picture, his simple answer was, 'I paint for eternity.' Do not be ashamed to be like him. Set your immortal soul before your mind's eye, and when men ask you why you live as you do, answer them in his spirit, 'I live for my soul.' Believe me, the day is fast coming when the soul will be the one thing men will think of, and the only question of importance will be this, *'Is my soul lost or saved?'*

(4) For another thing, *remember it is possible to be a young man and yet to serve God.*

I fear the snares that Satan lays for you on this point. I fear lest he succeed in filling your minds with the vain notion that to be a true Christian in youth is impossible. I have seen many carried away by this delusion. I have heard it said, 'You are requiring impossibilities in expecting so much religion from young people. Youth is no time for seriousness. Our desires are strong, and it was never intended that we should keep them under, as you wish us to do. God meant us to enjoy ourselves. There will be time enough for religion by and by.' And this kind of talk is only too much encouraged by the world. The world is only too ready to wink at youthful sins. The world appears to think it a matter of course that young men must

---

[20] Zeuxis, a Greek painter of Greece's golden age, 5th century BC.

'sow their wild oats'. The world seems to take it for granted young people *must* be irreligious, and that it is not possible for them to follow Christ.

Young men, I will ask you this simple question,—Where will you find anything of all this in the word of God? Where is the chapter or verse in the Bible, which will support this talking and reasoning of the world? Does not the Bible speak to old and young alike, without distinction? Is not sin, sin, whether committed at the age of twenty or fifty? Will it form the slightest excuse in the Day of Judgment to say, 'I know I sinned, but then I was young'? Show your common sense, I beg of you, by giving up such vain excuses. You are responsible and accountable to God from the very moment that you know right and wrong.

I know well there are many difficulties in a young man's way,—I allow it fully. But there are always difficulties in the way of doing right. The path to heaven is always narrow, whether we be young or old. There are difficulties, but God will give you grace to overcome them. God is no hard master. He will not, like Pharaoh, require you to make bricks without straw (Exod. 5:16). He will take care the path of plain duty is never impossible. He never laid commands on man which he would not give man power to perform (1 Cor. 10:13).

There are difficulties,—but many a young man has overcome them hitherto, and so may you. Moses was a young man of like passions with yourselves;—but see what is said of him in Scripture: 'By faith Moses, when he was come to years, refused to be called the son of Pharaoh's daughter; choosing rather to suffer affliction with the people of God, than to enjoy the pleasures of sin for a season; esteeming the reproach of Christ greater riches than the treasures of Egypt: for he had respect unto the recompence of the reward' (Heb. 11:24-26). Daniel was a young man when he began to serve God in Babylon. He was surrounded by temptations of every kind. He had few with him, and many against him. Yet Daniel's life was so blameless and consistent, that even his enemies could find no fault in him, except 'concerning the law of his God' (Dan. 6:5). And these are not solitary cases. There is a cloud of witnesses whom I could name. Time would fail me, if I were to tell you of young Isaac (Gen. 22), young Joseph (Gen. 39), young Joshua (Exod. 17:9-14), young Samuel (1 Sam. 2:18-3:21), young David (1 Sam. 16, 17), young Solomon (1 Kings 3:4-9), young Abijah (2 Chron. 13), young Obadiah (1 Kings 18:3), young Josiah (2 Chron. 34, 35), young Timothy (Acts 16:1-3). These were not angels, but men, with hearts naturally like your own. They too had obstacles to contend with, lusts to mortify, trials to endure, hard places to fill, like any of yourselves. But young as they were, they all found it possible to serve God. Will they not all rise in judgment and condemn you, if you persist in saying it cannot be done?

Young men, *try* to serve God. Resist the devil when he whispers it is impossible. Try,—and the Lord God of the promises will give you strength in the trying. He loves to meet those who struggle to come to him, and he will meet you and give you the power that you feel you need. Be like the man whom Bunyan's[21] Pilgrim saw in the Interpreter's house,—go forward boldly,

---

[21] John Bunyan (1628–88), Christian minister and gifted author whose most famous work, *The Pilgrim's Progress* (1678), depicts the Christian life in allegorical form.

saying, 'Set down my name.' Those words of our Lord are true, though I often hear them repeated by heartless and unfeeling tongues: 'Seek, and ye shall find; knock, and it shall be opened unto you' (Matt. 7:7). Difficulties which seemed like mountains shall melt away like snow in spring. Obstacles which seemed like giants in the mist of distance, shall dwindle into nothing when you fairly face them. The lion in the way which you fear, shall prove to be chained. If men believed the promises more, they would never be afraid of duties. But remember that little word I press upon you, and when Satan says, 'You cannot be a Christian while you are young': answer him, 'Get thee behind me, Satan: by God's help *I will try.*'

(5) For another thing, *determine as long as you live to make the Bible your guide and adviser.*

The Bible is God's merciful provision for sinful man's soul,—the map by which he must steer his course, if he would attain eternal life. All that we need to know, in order to make us peaceful, holy, or happy, is there richly contained. If a young man would know how to begin life well, let him hear what David says: 'Wherewithal shall a young man cleanse his way? by taking heed thereto according to thy word' (Psa. 119:9).

Young men, I charge you to make a habit of reading the Bible, and not to let the habit be broken. Let not the laughter of companions,—let not the bad customs of the family you may live in,—let none of these things prevent your doing it. Determine that you will not only *have* a Bible, but also make time to *read* it too. Suffer no man to persuade you that it is only a book for Sunday-school children and old women. It is the book from which King David got wisdom and understanding. It is the book which young Timothy knew from his childhood. Never be ashamed of reading it. Do not 'despise the word' (Prov. 13:13).

Read it *with prayer* for the Spirit's grace to make you understand it. Bishop Beveridge[22] says well, 'A man may as soon read the letter of Scripture without eyes, as understand the spirit of it without grace.'

Read it *reverently*, as the word of God, not of man,—believing implicitly that what it approves is right, and what it condemns is wrong. Be very sure that every doctrine which will not stand the test of Scripture is false. This will keep you from being tossed to and fro, and carried about by the dangerous opinions of these latter days. Be very sure that every *practice* in your life which is contrary to Scripture, is sinful and must be given up. This will settle many a question of conscience, and cut the knot of many a doubt. Remember how differently two kings of Judah read the word of God: Jehoiakim read it, and at once cut the writing to pieces, and burned it on the fire (Jer. 36:23). And why?—Because his heart rebelled against it, and he was resolved not to obey. Josiah read it, and at once rent his clothes, and cried mightily to the Lord (2 Chron. 34:19). And why?—Because his heart was tender and obedient. He was ready to do anything which Scripture showed him was his duty. Oh that you may follow the last of these two, and not the first!

[22] William Beveridge (1637–1708), a minister of the Church of England and later Bishop of Asaph, he was known as 'the great reviver and restorer of primitive piety'.

And *read it regularly*. This is the only way to become 'mighty in the Scriptures' (Acts 18:24). A hasty glance at the Bible now and then does little good. At that rate you will never become familiar with its treasures, or feel the sword of the Spirit fitted to your hand in the hour of conflict. But get your mind stored with Scripture, by diligent reading, and you will soon discover its value and power. Texts will rise up in your hearts in the moment of temptation. Commands will suggest themselves in seasons of doubt. Promises will come across your thoughts in the time of discouragement.—And thus you will experience the truth of David's words, 'Thy word have I hid in mine heart, that I might not sin against thee' (Psa. 119:11); and of Solomon's words, 'When thou goest, it shall lead thee; when thou sleepest, it shall keep thee; and when thou awakest, it shall talk with thee' (Prov. 6:22).

I dwell on these things more because this is an age of reading. Of making many books there seems no end, though few of them are really profitable. There seems a rage for cheap printing and publishing. Newspapers of every sort abound, and the tone of some, which have the widest circulation, tells badly for the taste of the age. Amidst the flood of dangerous reading, I plead for my Master's book,—I call upon you not to forget the book of the soul. Let not newspapers, novels, and romances be read, while the prophets and apostles lie despised. Let not the exciting and licentious swallow up your attention, while the edifying and the sanctifying can find no place in your mind.

Young men, give the Bible the honour due to it every day you live. Whatever you read, read that first. And beware of bad books: there are plenty in this day. Take heed what you read. I suspect there is more harm done to souls in this way than most people have an idea is possible. Value all books in proportion as they are agreeable to Scripture. Those that are nearest to it are the best, and those that are farthest from it, and most contrary to it, the worst.

(6) For another thing, *never make an intimate friend of anyone who is not a friend of God.*

Understand me,—I do not speak of *acquaintances*. I do not mean that you ought to have nothing to do with any but true Christians. To take such a line is neither possible nor desirable in this world. Christianity requires no man to be uncourteous.

But I do advise you to be very careful in your choice of *friends*. Do not open all your heart to a man merely because he is clever, agreeable, good-natured, high-spirited, and kind. These things are all very well in their way, but they are not everything. Never be satisfied with the friendship of anyone who will not be useful to your soul.

Believe me, the importance of this advice cannot be over-rated. There is no telling the harm that is done by associating with godless companions and friends. The devil has few better helps in ruining a man's soul. Grant him this help, and he cares little for all the armour with which you may be armed against him. Good education, early habits of morality, sermons, books, regular homes, letters of parents, all, he knows well, will avail you little if you cling to ungodly friends. You may resist many open temptations, refuse many plain snares; but once take up a bad companion, and he is content. That awful chapter which describes Amnon's wicked conduct about Tamar, almost begins with these words, 'But Amnon had a friend ... a very subtil man' (2 Sam. 13:3).

You must recollect, we are all creatures of imitation: precept may teach us, but it is example that draws us. There is that in us all, that we are always disposed to catch the ways of those with whom we live; and the more we like them, the stronger does the disposition grow. Without our being aware of it, they influence our tastes and opinions;—we gradually give up what they dislike, and take up what they like, in order to become more close friends with them. And, worst of all, we catch their ways in things that are wrong, far quicker than in things that are right. Health, unhappily, is not contagious, but disease is. It is far more easy to catch a chill than to impart a glow; and to make each other's religion dwindle away, than grow and prosper.

Young men, I ask you to lay these things to heart. Before you let anyone become your constant companion, before you get into the habit of telling him everything, and going to him in all your troubles and all your pleasures,—before you do this, just think of what I have been saying; ask yourself, 'Will this be a useful friendship to me or not?'

'Evil communications' do indeed 'corrupt good manners' (1 Cor. 15:33). I wish that text were written in hearts as often as it is in copy-books. Good friends are among our greatest blessings;—they may keep us back from much evil, quicken us in our course, speak a word in season, draw us upward, and draw us on. But a bad friend is a positive misfortune, a weight continually dragging us down, and chaining us to earth. Keep company with an irreligious man, and it is more than probable you will in the end become like him. That is the general consequence of all such friendships. The good go down to the bad, and the bad do not come up to the good. Even a stone will give way before a continual dropping. The world's proverb is only too correct: 'Clothes and company tell true tales about character.' 'Show me who a man lives with', say the Spaniards, 'and I will show you what he is.'

I dwell the more upon this point because it has more to do with your prospects in life than at first sight appears. If ever you marry, it is more than probable you will choose a wife among the connections of your friends. If Jehoshaphat's son Jehoram had not formed a friendship with Ahab's family, he would most likely not have married Ahab's daughter. And who can estimate the importance of a right choice in marriage? It is a step which, according to the old saying, 'either makes a man or mars him'. Your happiness in both lives may depend on it. Your wife must either help your soul or harm it: there is no medium. She will either fan the flame of religion in your heart, or throw cold water upon it, and make it burn low. She will either be wings or fetters, a rein or a spur to your Christianity, according to her character. He that findeth a good wife doth indeed 'findeth a good thing' (Prov. 18:22); but if you have the least wish to find one, be very careful how you choose your friends.

Do you ask me what kind of friends you shall choose? Choose friends who will benefit your soul,—friends whom you can really respect,—friends whom you would like to have near you on your death-bed,—friends who love the Bible and are not afraid to speak to you about it,—friends such as you will not be ashamed of owning at the coming of Christ, and at the day of judgment. Follow the example that David sets you: he says, 'I am a companion of all them that fear thee, and of them that keep thy precepts' (Psa. 119:63). Remember the words of Solomon: 'He that walketh with wise men shall be wise; but a companion of fools shall be destroyed' (Prov. 13:20). But depend on it, bad company in the life that now is, is the sure way to procure worse company in the life to come.

Part Four

Special Rules for Young Men

4. In the last place, *I will set down some particular rules of conduct, which I strongly advise all young men to follow.*

(1) For one thing, *resolve at once, by God's help, to break off every known sin, however small.*

Look within, each one of you. Examine your own hearts. Do you see there any habit or custom which you know to be wrong in the sight of God? If you do, delay not a moment in attacking it. Resolve at once to lay it aside.

Nothing darkens the eyes of the mind so much, and deadens the conscience so surely, as *an allowed sin*. It may be a little one, but it is not the less dangerous for all that. A small leak will sink a great ship, and a small spark will kindle a great fire, and a little allowed sin in like manner will ruin an immortal soul. Take my advice and never spare a little sin. Israel was commanded to slay every Canaanite, both great and small. Act on the same principle, and show no mercy to little sins. Well says the Song of Solomon, 'Take us the foxes, the *little* foxes, that spoil the vines' (Song of Sol. 2:15).

Be sure no wicked man ever meant to be so wicked at his first beginnings. But he began with allowing himself some *little* transgression, and that led on to something greater, and that in time produced something greater still, and thus he became the miserable being that he now is. When Hazael heard from Elisha of the horrible acts that he would one day do, he said with astonishment, 'Is thy servant a dog, that he should do this great thing?' (2 Kings 8:13). But he allowed sin to take root in his heart, and in the end he did them all.

Young men, resist sin in its beginnings. They may look small and insignificant, but mind what I say, resist them,—make no compromise, let no sin lodge quietly and undisturbed in your heart. 'The mother of mischief,' says an old proverb, 'is no bigger than a midge's wing.' There is nothing finer than the point of a needle, but when it has made a hole, it draws all the thread after it. Remember the apostle's words, 'A little leaven leaveneth the whole lump' (1 Cor. 5:6).

Many a young man could tell you with sorrow and shame, that he traces the ruin of all his worldly prospects to the point I speak of,—to giving way to sin in its beginnings. He began habits of falsehood and dishonesty in little things, and they grew upon him. Step by step, he has gone on from bad to worse, till he has done things that at one time he would have thought impossible; till at last he has lost his place, lost his character, lost his comfort, and well-nigh lost his soul. He allowed a gap in the wall of his conscience, because it seemed a little one,—and once allowed, that gap grew larger every day, till at length the whole wall seemed to come down.

Remember this especially in matters of *truth* and *honesty*. Make conscience of pins[23] and syllables. 'He that is faithful in that which is least, is faithful also in much' (Luke 16:10). Whatever the world may please to say, there are no little sins. All great buildings are made up of little parts;—the first stone is as important as any other. All habits are formed by a succession of little acts, and the first little act is of mighty consequence. The axe in the fable only begged the trees to let him have one little piece of wood to make a handle, and he would never trouble them any more. He got it, and then he soon cut them all down. The devil only wants to get the wedge of a little allowed sin into your heart, and you will soon be all his own. It is a wise saying of old William Bridge,[24] 'There is nothing small betwixt us and God, for God is an infinite God.'

There are two ways of coming down from the top of a church steeple; one is to jump down,—and the other is to come down by the steps: but both will lead you to the bottom. So also there are two ways of going to hell; one is to walk into it with your eyes open,—few people do that; the other is to go down by the steps of little sins,—and that way, I fear, is only too common. Put up with a few little sins, and you will soon want a few more. Even a heathen[25] could say, 'Who ever was content with only one sin?' And then your course will be regularly worse and worse every year. Well did Jeremy Taylor[26] describe the progress

---

[23] Pins: *i.e.*, small, insignificant things.

[24] William Bridge (c. 1637–1708), a leading English Puritan minister, preacher, and writer, his best known work being *A Lifting Up for the Downcast*.

[25] Juvenal (34 BC–AD 12), a Roman satirical poet.

[26] Jeremy Taylor (1613–67), a minister of the Church of England, Bishop of Down

of sin in a man: 'First it startles him, then it becomes pleasing, then easy, then delightful, then frequent, then habitual, then confirmed!—then the man is impenitent, then obstinate, then resolves never to repent, and then he is damned.'

Young men, if you would not come to this, recollect the rule I give you this day,—resolve at once to break off every known sin.

(2) For another thing, *resolve, by God's help, to shun everything which may prove an occasion for sin.*

It is an excellent saying of good Bishop Hall,[27] 'He that would be safe from the acts of evil, must widely avoid the occasions.'[28] It is not enough that we determine to commit no sin, we must carefully keep at a distance from all approaches to it. By this test we ought to try our ways of spending our time,—the books that we read, the families that we visit, the society into which we go. We must not content ourselves with saying, 'There is nothing positively wrong here'; we must go further, and say, 'Is there anything here which may prove to me the occasion of sin?'

This, be it remembered, is one great reason why *idleness* is so much to be avoided. It is not that doing nothing is of itself so positively wicked; it is the opportunity it affords to evil thoughts, and vain imaginations; it is the wide door it opens

---

and Connor, and vice-chancellor of the University of Dublin, best known for his twin devotional manual, *Holy Living and Holy Dying* (1650, 1651).

[27] Joseph Hall (1574–1656), Church of England Bishop of Norwich.

[28] There is an old fable, that the butterfly once asked the owl how she should deal with the fire, which had singed her wings; and the owl counselled her, in reply, not to behold so much as its smoke.

for Satan to throw in the seeds of bad things; it is this which is mainly to be feared. If David had not given occasion to the devil, by idling on his house-top at Jerusalem, he would probably never have seen Bathsheba, nor murdered Uriah.

This, too, is one great reason why *worldly amusements* are so objectionable. It may be difficult, in some instances, to show that they are, in themselves, positively unscriptural and wrong. But there is little difficulty in showing that the *tendency* of almost all of them is most injurious to the soul. They sow the seeds of an earthly and sensual frame of mind. They war against the life of faith. They promote an unhealthy and unnatural craving after excitement. They minister to the lust of the flesh, and the lust of the eye, and the pride of life (1 John 2:16). They dim the view of heaven and eternity, and give a false colour to the things of time. They indispose the heart for private prayer, Scripture-reading, and calm communion with God. The man who mingles in them is like one who gives Satan vantage-ground. He has a battle to fight, and he gives his enemy the help of sun, wind, and hill. It would be strange indeed if he did not find himself continually overcome.

Young men, endeavour, as much as in you lies, to keep clear of everything which may prove injurious to your soul. Never hold a candle to the devil. People may say you are over scrupulous, too particular, where is the mighty harm of such and such things? But heed them not. It is dangerous to play tricks with edged tools: it is far more dangerous to take liberties with your immortal soul. He that would be safe must not come near the brink of danger. He must look on his heart as a magazine of gunpowder, and be cautious not to handle one spark of temptation more than he can help.

Where is the use of your praying, 'Lead us not into temptation' (Matt. 6:13), unless you are yourselves careful not to run into it; and 'deliver us from evil', unless you show a desire to keep out of its way? Take example from Joseph,—Not merely did he refuse his mistress's solicitation to sin, but he showed his prudence in refusing to be 'with her' at all (Gen. 39:10). Lay to heart the advice of Solomon, not merely to 'go not in the path of wickedness', but to 'avoid it, pass not by it, turn from it, and pass away' (Prov. 4:15); not merely not to be drunken, but not even to '*look* upon the wine when it is red' (Prov. 23:31). The man who took the vow of a Nazarite in Israel not only took no wine, but he even abstained from grapes in any shape whatever. '*Abhor* that which is evil', says Paul to the Romans (Rom. 12:9); not merely do not do it;—'*Flee* youthful lusts', he writes to Timothy; get away from them as far as possible (2 Tim. 2:22). Alas, how needful are such cautions! Dinah must needs go out among the wicked Shechemites, to see their ways, and she lost her character. Lot must needs pitch his tent near sinful Sodom, and he lost everything but his life.

Young men, be wise in time. Do not be always trying how near you can allow the enemy of souls to come, and yet escape him. Hold him at arm's length. Try to keep clear of temptation as far as possible, and this will be one great help to keep clear of sin.

(3) For another thing, *resolve never to forget the eye of God.*

The eye of God! Think of that. Everywhere, in every house, in every field, in every room, in every company, alone or in a crowd, the eye of God is always upon you. 'The eyes of the LORD are in every place, beholding the evil and the good' (Prov. 15:3), and they are eyes that read hearts as well as actions.

Endeavour, I beseech you all, to realize this fact. Recollect that you have to do with an all-seeing God,—a God who never slumbereth nor sleepeth (Psa. 121:4),—a God who understands your thoughts afar off, and with whom the night shines as the day (Psa. 139:2, 12). You may leave your father's roof, and go away, like the prodigal into a far country (Luke 15:13), and think that there is nobody to watch your conduct; but the eye and ear of God are there before you. You may deceive your parents or employers, you may tell them falsehoods and be one thing before their faces, and another behind their backs, but you cannot deceive God. He knows you through and through. He heard what you said as you came here today. He knows what you are thinking of at this minute. He has set your most secret sins in the light of his countenance, and they will one day come out before the world to your shame, except you take heed (1 Cor. 4:5).

How little is this really felt! How many things are done continually, which men would never do if they thought they were seen! How many matters are transacted in the chambers of imagination, which would never bear the light of day! Yes; men entertain thoughts in private, and say words in private, and do acts in private, which they would be ashamed and blush to have exposed before the world. The sound of a footstep coming has stopped many a deed of wickedness. A knock at the door has caused many an evil work to be hastily suspended and hurriedly laid aside. But oh, what miserable drivelling folly is all this! There is an all-seeing Witness with us wherever we go. Lock the door, draw down the blind, shut the shutters, put out the candle; it matters not, it makes no difference; God is everywhere, you cannot shut him out, or prevent his seeing. 'All things are naked and open unto the eyes of him with whom we have to do' (Heb. 4:13). Well did young Joseph understand this when his mistress tempted him. There was no one in the house to see them,—no human eye to witness against him;—but Joseph was one who lived as seeing him that is invisible: 'How can I do this great wickedness', said he, 'and sin against God?' (Gen. 39:9).

Young men, I ask you all to read Psalm 139. I advise you all to learn it by heart. Make it the test of all your dealings in this world's business: say to yourself often, 'Do I remember that God sees me?'

Live as in the sight of God. This is what Abraham did,—he walked *before* him. This is what Enoch did,—he walked *with* him. This is what heaven itself will be,—the eternal presence of God. *Do* nothing you would not like God to see. *Say* nothing you would not like God to hear. *Write* nothing you would not like God to read. *Go* to no place where you would not like God to find you. *Read* no book of which you would not like God to say, 'Show it me.' Never spend your time in such a way that you would not like to have God say, 'What art thou doing?'

(4) For another thing, *be diligent in the use of all public means of grace.*

Be regular in going to the house of God, whenever it is open for prayer and preaching, and it is in your power to attend. Be regular in keeping the Lord's day holy, and determine that God's day out of the seven shall henceforth always be given to its rightful owner.

I would not leave any false impression on your minds. Do not go away and say I told you that keeping your church made up the whole of religion. I tell you no such thing. I have no wish to see you grow up formalists and Pharisees. If you think the mere carrying your body to a certain house, at certain times, on a certain day in the week, will make you a Christian, and prepare you to meet God, I tell you flatly you are miserably deceived. All services without heart service are unprofitable and vain. They only are true worshippers who worship God 'in spirit and in truth: the Father seeketh such to worship him' (John 4:23).

But means of grace are not to be despised because they are not saviours. Gold is not food; you cannot eat it,—but you would not therefore say it is useless and throw it away. Your soul's eternal well-doing most certainly does not depend on means of grace, but it is no less certain that without them, as a general rule, your soul will not do well. God *might* take all who are saved to heaven in a chariot of fire, as he did Elijah, but he does not do so. He *might* teach them all by visions, and dreams, and miraculous interpositions, without requiring them to read or think for themselves, but he does not do so. And why not?

Because he is a God that works by means, and it is his law and will that in all man's dealings with him means shall be used. None but a fool or enthusiast would think of building a house without ladders and scaffolding, and just so no wise man will despise means.

I dwell the more on this point, because Satan will try hard to fill your minds with arguments against means. He will draw your attention to the numbers of persons who use them and are no better for the using. 'See there', he will whisper, 'do you not observe those who go to church are no better than those who stay away?' But do not let this move you. It is never fair to argue against a thing because it is improperly used. It does not follow that means of grace can do no good because many attend on them and get no good from them. Medicine is not to be despised because many take it and do not recover their health. No man would think of giving up eating and drinking because others choose to eat and drink improperly, and so make themselves ill. The value of means of grace, like other things, depends in a great measure on the manner and spirit in which we use them.

I dwell on this point too, because of the strong anxiety I feel that every young man should regularly hear the preaching of Christ's gospel. I cannot tell you how important I think this is. By God's blessing, the ministry of the gospel might be the means of converting your soul,—of leading you to a saving knowledge of Christ,—of making you a child of God in deed and in truth. This would be cause for eternal thankfulness indeed. This would be an event over which angels would rejoice. But even if this were not the case, there is a *restraining* power and influence in the ministry of the gospel, under which I earnestly desire every young man to be brought. There are thousands whom it keeps back from evil, though it has not yet turned them unto God;—it has made them far better members of society, though it has not yet made them true Christians. There is a certain kind of mysterious power in the faithful preaching of the gospel, which tells insensibly on multitudes who listen to it without receiving it into their hearts. To hear sin cried down, and holiness cried up, to hear Christ exalted, and the works of the devil denounced,—to hear the kingdom of heaven and its blessedness described, and the world and its emptiness exposed; to hear this week after week, Sunday after Sunday, is seldom without good effect to the soul. It makes it far harder afterwards to run into any excess of riot and profligacy. It acts as a wholesome check upon a man's heart. This, I believe, is one way in which that promise of God is made good, 'My word shall not return unto me void' (Isa. 55:11). There is much truth in that strong saying of Whitefield, 'The gospel keeps many a one from the gaol and gallows, if it does not keep him from hell.'

Let me here name another point which is closely connected with this subject. Let nothing ever tempt you to become a Sabbath-breaker. I press this on your attention. Make conscience of giving all your Sabbath[29] to God. A spirit of disregard for this

---

[29] The Christian Sabbath or Lord's day is the first day of the week (Sunday) and is to be kept holy: 'The Sabbath is to be sanctified by a holy resting all that day, even from such worldly employments and recreations as are lawful on other days; and spending

holy day is growing up amongst us with fearful rapidity, and not least among young men. Sunday travelling by railways and steamboats, Sunday visiting, Sunday excursions, are becoming every year more common than they were, and are doing infinite harm to souls.

Young men, be jealous on this point. Whether you live in town or country, take up a decided line; resolve not to profane your Sabbath. Let not this plausible argument of 'needful relaxation for your body',—let not the example of all around you,—let not the invitation of companions with whom you may be thrown;—let none of these things move you to depart from this settled rule, that *God's day shall be given to God*.

Once give over caring for the Sabbath, and in the end you will give over caring for your soul. The steps which lead to this conclusion are easy and regular. Begin with not honouring God's day, and you will soon not honour God's house;—cease to honour God's house, and you will soon cease to honour God's book; cease to honour God's book, and by and by you will give God no honour at all. Let a man lay the foundation of having *no Sabbath*, and I am never surprised if he finishes with the top-stone of *no God*. It is a remarkable saying of Judge Hale,[30] 'Of all the persons who were convicted of capital crimes[31] while he was upon the bench, he found only a few who would not confess, on inquiry, that they began their career of wickedness by a neglect of the Sabbath.'

---

the whole time in the public and private exercises of God's worship, except so much as is to be taken up in the works of necessity and mercy.' *Shorter Catechism*, Q&A 60.

[30] Sir Matthew Hale (1609–76), an influential English barrister, judge, and lawyer.

[31] Crimes that can result in a death penalty are known as capital crimes.

Young men, you may be thrown among companions who forget the honour of the Lord's day; but resolve, by God's help, that you will always remember to keep it holy. Honour it by a regular attendance at some place where the gospel is preached. Settle down under a faithful ministry, and once settled, let your place in church never be empty. Believe me, you will find a special blessing following you: 'If thou call the Sabbath a delight, the holy of the Lord, honourable; and shalt honour him, not doing thine own ways, nor finding thine own pleasure, nor speaking thine own words: then shalt thou delight thyself in the Lord; and I will cause thee to ride upon the high places of the earth' (Isa. 58:13, 14). And one thing is very certain,—your feelings about the Sabbath will always be a test and criterion of your fitness for heaven. Sabbaths are a foretaste and fragment of heaven. The man who finds them a burden and not a privilege, may be sure that his heart stands in need of a mighty change.

(5) For another thing, *resolve that wherever you are, you will pray.*

Prayer is the life-breath of a man's soul. Without it, we may have a name to live, and be counted Christians; but we are dead in the sight of God. The feeling that we must cry to God for mercy and peace is a mark of grace; and the habit of spreading before him our soul's wants is an evidence that we have the spirit of adoption. And prayer is the appointed way to obtain the relief of our spiritual necessities.—It opens the treasury, and sets the fountain flowing. If we have not, it is because we ask not.

Prayer is the way to procure the outpouring of the Spirit upon our hearts. Jesus has promised the Holy Ghost, the Comforter. He is ready to come down with all his precious gifts, renewing, sanctifying, purifying, strengthening, cheering, encouraging, enlightening, teaching, directing, guiding into all truth. But then he waits to be entreated.

And here it is, I say it with sorrow, here it is that men fall short so miserably. Few indeed are to be found who pray: many who go down on their knees, and say a form perhaps, but few who pray; few who cry unto God, few who call upon the Lord, few who seek as if they wanted to find, few who knock as if they hungered and thirsted, few who wrestle, few who strive with God earnestly for an answer, few who give him no rest, few who continue in prayer, few who watch unto prayer, few who pray always without ceasing and faint not. Yes: few pray! It is just one of the things assumed as a matter of course, but seldom practised; a thing which is everybody's business, but in fact hardly anybody performs.

Young men, believe me, if your soul is to be saved, you must pray. God has no dumb children. If you are to resist the world, the flesh, and the devil (1 John 2:16), you must pray: it is in vain to look for strength in the hour of trial, if it has not been sought for. You may be thrown with those who never do it, you may have to sleep in the same room with someone who never asks anything of God,—still, mark my words, you must pray.

I can quite believe you find great difficulties about it, difficulties about opportunities, and seasons, and places. I dare not lay

68

down too positive rules on such points as these. I leave them to your own conscience. You must be guided by circumstances. Our Lord Jesus Christ prayed on a mountain; Isaac prayed in the fields; Hezekiah turned his face to the wall as he lay upon his bed; Daniel prayed by the riverside; Peter, the apostle, on the house-top. I have heard of young men praying in stables and hay-lofts. All that I contend for is this,—you must know what it is to 'enter into thy closet' (Matt. 6:6). There must be stated times when you must speak to God face to face,—you must every day have your seasons for prayer.—*You must pray.*

Without this, all advice and counsel is useless. This is that piece of spiritual armour which Paul names last in his catalogue in Ephesians 6, but it is in truth first in value and importance. This is that meat which you must daily eat, if you would travel safely through the wilderness of this life. It is only in the strength of this that you will get onward towards the mount of God. I have heard it said that the needle-grinders of Shef-field sometimes wear a magnetic mouthpiece at their work, which catches all the fine dust that flies around them, prevents it entering their lungs, and so saves their lives. Prayer is the mouthpiece that you must wear continually, or else you will never work on uninjured by the unhealthy atmosphere of this sinful world.—*You must pray.*

Young men, be assured of this: no time is so well spent as that which a man spends upon his knees. Make time for this, whatever your employment may be. Think of David, king of Israel: what does he say? 'Evening, and morning, and at noon will I pray and cry aloud, and he shall hear my voice' (Psa. 55:17). Think of Daniel. He had all the business of a kingdom on his hands; yet he prayed three times a day. See there the secret of his safety in wicked Babylon. Think of Solomon. He begins his reign with prayer for help and assistance, and hence his wonderful prosperity. Think of Nehemiah. He could find time to pray to the God of heaven, even when standing in the presence of his master, Artaxerxes. Think of the example these godly men have left you, and go and do likewise.

Oh, that the Lord may give you all the spirit of grace and supplication! 'Wilt thou not from this time cry unto me, My father, thou art the guide of my youth?' (Jer. 3:4). Gladly would I consent that all this address should be forgotten, if only this doctrine of the importance of prayer might be impressed on your hearts.

Conclusion

And now I hasten towards a conclusion. I have said things that many perhaps will not like, and not receive; but I appeal to your consciences, *Are they not true?*

Young men, you all have consciences. Corrupt and ruined by the Fall as we are, each of us has a conscience. In a corner of each heart there sits a witness for God,—a witness who condemns when we do wrong and approves when we do right. To that witness I make my appeal this day, *Are not the things that I have been saying true?*

Go then, young men, and resolve this day to remember your Creator in the days of your youth. Before the day of grace is past,—before your conscience has become hardened by age and deadened by repeated trampling under foot,—while you have strength, and time, and opportunities,—go and join yourself to the Lord in an everlasting covenant not to be forgotten. The Spirit will not always strive. The voice of conscience will become feebler and fainter every year you continue to resist it. The Athenians said to Paul, 'We will hear thee again of this matter', but they had heard him for the last time (Acts 17:32). Make haste and delay not. Linger and hesitate no more.

Think of the unspeakable *comfort you will give to parents*, relations, and friends, if you take my counsel. They have expended time, money, and health to rear you and make you what you are. Surely they deserve some consideration at your hands. Who can reckon up the joy and gladness which young people have it in their power to occasion? Who can tell the anxiety and sorrow that sons like Esau (Gen. 25-27), and Hophni and Phinehas (1 Sam. 1-4), and Absalom (2 Sam. 13) may cause? Truly indeed does Solomon say, 'A wise son maketh a glad father, but a foolish son is the heaviness of his mother' (Prov. 10:1). Oh, consider these things, and give God your heart! Let it not be said of you at last, as it is of many, that your 'youth was a blunder, your manhood a struggle, and your old age a regret'.

Think of the *good you may be as the instrument of doing good to the world*. Almost all the most eminent saints of God sought the Lord early. Moses, Samuel, David, Daniel, all served God from their youth. God seems to delight in putting special honour upon young servants;—remember the honour he placed upon our own young king, Edward VI. And what might we not confidently expect, if young men in our own day would consecrate the spring-time of their lives to God? Agents are wanted now in almost every great and good cause, and cannot be found. Machinery of every kind for spreading truth exists, but there are not hands to work it. Money is more easily got for doing good than men. Ministers are wanted for new churches,—missionaries are wanted for new stations,—visitors are wanted for neglected districts,—teachers are wanted for new schools;—many a good cause is standing still merely for want of agents. The supply of godly, faithful, trustworthy men, for posts like those I have named, is far below the demand.

Young men of the present day, *you are wanted for God*. This is peculiarly an age of activity. We are shaking off some of our past selfishness. Men no longer sleep the sleep of apathy and indifference about others, as their forefathers did. They are beginning to be ashamed of thinking like Cain,—'Am I my brother's keeper?' (Gen. 4:9). A wide field of usefulness is open before you, if you are only willing to enter upon it. The harvest is great but the labourers are few (Luke 10:2). Be zealous of good works. Come, come to the cause of the Lord against the mighty.

This is, in some sort, to be like God, not only 'good, but doing good' (Psa. 119:68). This is the way to follow the steps of your Lord and Saviour: 'He went about doing good' (Acts 10:38).

This is to live as David did; he 'served his own generation' (Acts 13:36).

And who can doubt that this is the path which most becomes an immortal soul? Who would not rather leave this world like Josiah, lamented by all, than depart like Jehoram, 'without being desired'? (2 Chron. 21:20). Whether is it better to be an idle, frivolous, useless cumberer of the ground, to live for your body, your selfishness, your lusts, and your pride,—or to spend and be spent in the glorious cause of usefulness to your fellow men;—to be like Wilberforce[32] or Lord Shaftesbury,[33] a blessing to your country and the world,—to be like Howard,[34] the friend of the prisoner and the captive,—to be like Schwartz,[35] the spiritual father of hundreds of immortal souls in heathen lands,—to be like that man of God, Robert M'Cheyne,[36] a burning and a shining light, an epistle of Christ, known and read of all men, the quickener of every Christian heart that comes across your path? Oh, who can doubt? Who can for one moment doubt?

Young men, consider your responsibilities. Think of the privilege and luxury of doing good. Resolve this day to be useful. At once, give your hearts to Christ.

Think, lastly, of the *happiness* that will come to your own soul, if you serve God,—happiness by the way, as you travel through life,—and happiness in the end, when the journey is over. Believe me, whatever vain notions you may have heard, believe me, there is a reward for the righteous even in this world. Godliness has indeed the promise of this life, as well as of that which is to come. There is a solid peace in feeling that God is your friend. There is a real satisfaction in knowing that however great your unworthiness, you are complete in Christ,—that you

---

[32] William Wilberforce (1759–1833), English statesman and philanthropist. He led the movement to abolish the British slave trade. He died shortly before the legislation passed Parliament that abolished slavery in most of the British Empire.

[33] Lord Shaftesbury (1801–85), Anthony Ashley Cooper, 7th Earl of Shaftesbury was an English politician, philanthropist, and social reformer.

[34] John Howard (1726–90), English philanthropist and pioneering prison reformer.

[35] Christian F. Schwartz (1726–98), German Lutheran Protestant missionary to India.

[36] Robert Murray M'Cheyne (1813–43), minister of the Church of Scotland, whose brief but godly life made a lasting impact on those who knew him.

have an enduring portion,—that you have chosen that good part which shall not be taken from you.

The backslider in heart may well be filled with his own ways, but 'a good man shall be satisfied from himself' (Prov. 14:14). The path of the worldly man grows darker and darker every year that he lives;—the path of the Christian is as a shining light, brighter and brighter to the very end. His sun is just rising when the sun of the worldly is setting for ever;—his best things are all beginning to blossom and bloom for ever, when those of the worldly are all slipping out of his hands, and passing away.

Young men, these things are true. Suffer the word of exhortation. Be persuaded. Take up the cross. Follow Christ. Yield yourselves unto God.

THE END

Other J. C. Ryle Titles
published by
The Banner of Truth Trust

Booklets

The Agency that Transformed a Nation
ISBN: 978-1-84871-115-0, 16pp.

A Call to Prayer
ISBN: 978-0-85151-819-0, 32pp.

Simplicity in Preaching
ISBN: 978-1-84871-065-8, 24pp.

Worship: Its Priority, Principles, and Practice
ISBN: 978-0-85151-906-7, 32pp.

'[Ryle's writings are] a distillation of true Puritan theology presented in a highly readable and modern form.'

Martyn Lloyd-Jones

Paperback Books

Warnings to the Churches
ISBN: 978-0-85151-043-9

Is All Scripture Inspired?
ISBN: 978-0-85151-848-0, 80pp.

Five English Reformers
ISBN: 978-0-85151-138-2, 232pp.

Christian Leaders of the Eighteenth Century
ISBN: 978-0-85151-268-6

The Upper Room: Being a Few Truths for the Times
ISBN: 978-0-85151-376-8

'I see [Ryle] as a single-minded Christian communicator of
profound biblical, theological, and practical wisdom, a man
and minister of giant personal stature and electric force
of utterance that sympathetic readers still feel.'

J. I. PACKER

Clothbound Books

Expository Thoughts on the Gospels, 7 vols.
ISBN: 978-1-84871-136-5

Holiness: Its Nature, Hindrances, Difficulties and Roots
ISBN: 978-1-84871-506-6, 480pp.

Light from Old Times: or, Protestant Facts and Men
ISBN: 978-1-84871-636-0, 432pp.

*Old Paths: Being Plain Statements on Some of the
Weightier Matters of Christianity*
ISBN: 978-1-84871-227-0, 408pp.

*Practical Religion: Being Plain Papers on the Duties,
Experience, Dangers, and Privileges of Professing Christians*
ISBN: 978-1-84871-224-9

*'Ryle is magnificent! There's no other word for it. He packs more
experience and sanctified common sense into two dozen pages
than many others manage in a lengthy treatise.'*

Sinclair B. Ferguson

Some other
Banner of Truth Trust
publications

Sermons on Titus
John Calvin
Translated from the original French by Robert White

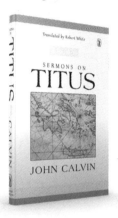

ISBN: 978-1-84871-569-1, 312pp., clothbound

While the seventeen sermons in this volume were preached by
Calvin between August and mid-October, 1555 during the course
of his regular pulpit ministry in Geneva, they are far from being
mere historical curiosities. Along with concern for irreproachable
leadership, faithful teaching, and the spiritual well-being of the
church's members, the apostle's letter to Titus sounds a strongly
ethical and evangelistic note in its emphasis on upright living, by
which God is honoured and outsiders are drawn to the faith as
they witness the power and grace of the gospel.

The Banner of Truth
monthly magazine

The Banner of Truth magazine is published monthly by The Banner of Truth Trust, 11 issues per year with a double issue normally appearing in August/September, and in electronic form as a portable document format (pdf) file.

The magazine aims at a serious approach to the Christian faith by means of devotional, historical, and doctrinal studies, and seeks to show how that faith relates to modern issues and attitudes. 'News & Comment' and 'Book Reviews' sections are also included.

The Banner of Truth Trust originated in 1957 in London. The founders believed that much of the best literature of historic Christianity had been allowed to fall into oblivion and that, under God, its recovery could well lead not only to a strengthening of the church, but to true revival.

Interdenominational in vision, this publishing work is now international, and our lists include a number of contemporary authors along with classics from the past. The translation of these books into many languages is encouraged.

A monthly magazine, *The Banner of Truth*, is also published. More information about this and all our publications can be found on our website or supplied by either of the offices below.

THE BANNER OF TRUTH TRUST

3 Murrayfield Road
Edinburgh, EH12 6EL
UK

PO Box 621, Carlisle,
Pennsylvania 17013
USA

www.banneroftruth.org